Bountiful Bolognese

A Culinary Journey Through Perfect Pasta Sauces

While every precaution has been taken in the preparation of this book, the publisher assumes no responsibility for errors or omissions, or for damages resulting from the use of the information contained herein.

BOUNTIFUL BOLOGNESE

First edition. December 15, 2023.

ISBN: 979-8223269281

Written by Jose Maria.

Table of Contents

Jose Maria

I. Introduction

A. Brief History of Bolognese Sauce

The origins of Bolognese sauce can be traced back to the city of Bologna in Northern Italy. Also known as "Ragù alla Bolognese," this savory meat-based sauce has a rich culinary history. Legend has it that the sauce dates back to the 18th century and was created by the skilled chefs of Bologna. Originally, Bolognese sauce was a slow-cooked meat sauce, often paired with fresh pasta.

B. The Art of Perfecting Pasta

To complement the hearty and flavorful Bolognese sauce, mastering the art of cooking pasta is essential. Here are some key tips:

Choosing Quality Pasta: Select high-quality pasta made from durum wheat for better texture and flavor.

Salted Boiling Water: Add a generous amount of salt to boiling water before cooking pasta. This enhances the pasta's natural flavor.

Al Dente Perfection: Cook pasta al dente, which means it should be firm to the bite. This ensures a satisfying texture.

Reserve Pasta Water: Before draining the pasta, reserve a

small cup of the cooking water. This starchy water can be added to the sauce to adjust its consistency and help it adhere better to the pasta.

Timing is Crucial: Coordinate the pasta cooking time with the completion of the sauce. Ideally, the pasta should be ready just as the Bolognese sauce reaches its peak flavor.

C. Essential Ingredients and Tools

To create the perfect Bolognese sauce, assemble the following ingredients and tools:

Ingredients:

Ground Meat Selection:

- High-quality ground beef and pork mixture (traditional)
- Optional: Ground veal for a luxurious touch

Aromatic Vegetables:

- Onion, finely chopped
- Carrots, finely chopped
- Celery, finely chopped

Tomato Varieties:

- San Marzano tomatoes (canned or fresh)
- Tomato paste for depth of flavor

Herbs and Spices:

- Fresh basil and oregano (or dried if fresh is unavailable)
- Bay leaves
- Salt and black pepper to taste

Tools:

Heavy-Duty Pot:

- For slow simmering the sauce to perfection.

Wooden Spoon:

- Ideal for stirring and ensuring even cooking.

Chef's Knife:

- Essential for finely chopping aromatic vegetables.

Grater:

- For grating fresh Parmesan cheese as a finishing touch.

Pasta Pot:

- A large pot for cooking pasta.

Colander:

- To drain the cooked pasta efficiently.

Measuring Cups and Spoons:

- For precise ingredient measurements.

Large Mixing Bowl:

- If preparing homemade pasta.

Equipped with these ingredients and tools, you're ready to embark on a culinary journey through the world of Bolognese sauce and perfect pasta pairings.

II. Classic Bolognese Recipe

A. Ingredients

Ground Meat Selection:

- 1 lb high-quality ground beef
- 1/2 lb ground pork (or a mixture of beef, pork, and veal)
- Optional: 1/4 lb ground veal

Aromatic Vegetables:

- 1 large onion, finely chopped
- 2 carrots, finely chopped
- 2 celery stalks, finely chopped

Tomato Varieties:

- 1 can (28 oz) San Marzano tomatoes, crushed
- 2 tablespoons tomato paste

Herbs and Spices:

- 2 bay leaves
- 2 sprigs fresh basil or 1 teaspoon dried basil
- 1 teaspoon dried oregano
- Salt and black pepper to taste

B. Cooking Techniques

Sautéing and Browning:

a. In a heavy-duty pot, heat olive oil over medium heat.

b. Add finely chopped onions, carrots, and celery. Sauté until softened and aromatic.

c. Add ground meats, breaking them apart with a wooden spoon. Cook until browned.

Slow Simmering:

a. Stir in tomato paste and cook for 2 minutes.

b. Pour in crushed San Marzano tomatoes, add bay leaves, basil, oregano, salt, and black pepper.

c. Reduce heat to low, cover, and let the sauce simmer for at least 2 hours, stirring occasionally.

C. Tips for Achieving Depth of Flavor

1. **Quality Ingredients:** Use the best quality meats and tomatoes for a rich flavor profile.
2. **Patient Simmering:** Allow the sauce to simmer slowly. This enhances the melding of flavors and creates a depth characteristic of Bolognese.
3. **Seasoning:** Taste and adjust salt and pepper throughout the cooking process. A pinch of sugar can also balance acidity.

D. Serving Suggestions

Serve the Classic Bolognese over a bed of al dente pasta, such as tagliatelle or pappardelle. Finish with a sprinkle of freshly grated Parmesan cheese and a few basil leaves. Consider pairing with a robust red wine, such as Chianti. For a complete meal, accompany it with a simple green salad and crusty garlic bread.

Enjoy the rich, comforting flavors of this timeless Bolognese sauce!

III. Variations on the Classic
A. Vegetarian Bolognese

Plant-based Protein Options:

- 1 lb plant-based ground meat (soy, tempeh, or mushroom-based alternatives)
- 1/2 cup red lentils (rinsed and drained)

Hearty Vegetables:

- 1 large onion, finely chopped
- 2 carrots, finely chopped
- 2 celery stalks, finely chopped
- 1 zucchini, diced
- 1 bell pepper, diced

Follow the same cooking techniques as the Classic Bolognese, substituting plant-based protein and lentils. Adjust cooking times as needed.

B. Seafood Twist

Fresh Seafood Selection:

- 1/2 lb shrimp, peeled and deveined
- 1/2 lb mussels, cleaned and debearded
- 1/2 lb white fish fillets, cut into bite-sized pieces

Lighter Tomato Base:

- 1 can (14 oz) diced tomatoes (drained)
- 1/2 cup seafood broth or dry white wine

Cooking Techniques:
a. Sauté onions, carrots, and celery as in the Classic Bolognese.
b. Add seafood and cook until shrimp turns pink and mussels open.
c. Pour in diced tomatoes and seafood broth or wine. Simmer until the sauce thickens.

C. Chicken Bolognese

Ground Chicken Tips:

- 1 lb ground chicken
- 1/2 lb ground turkey for added flavor

Complementary Flavors:

- 1 teaspoon smoked paprika
- 1/2 teaspoon dried thyme
- 1/2 cup dry white wine

Cooking Techniques:
a. Sauté onions, carrots, and celery until softened.
b. Add ground chicken and turkey. Cook until browned.
c. Stir in smoked paprika, dried thyme, and white wine. Simmer until the sauce thickens.

Adjust seasoning and herbs according to taste. Serve each variation over your favorite pasta, and garnish with appropriate herbs and cheeses. Enjoy exploring the diverse flavors of Bolognese!

IV. Perfect Pasta Pairings

A. Choosing the Right Pasta Shape

Tagliatelle:

Ideal for Classic Bolognese; its broad, flat surface captures the richness of the sauce.

Pappardelle:

A wider pasta that works well with the hearty texture of both Classic and Vegetarian Bolognese.

Fettuccine:

Another broad pasta choice that complements the robust flavors of Bolognese.

Linguine:

Suitable for a Seafood Twist, allowing the seafood and lighter sauce to coat the pasta.

Rigatoni:

Works with any Bolognese variation, providing pockets for the sauce to cling to.

B. Cooking Pasta Al Dente

Salted Boiling Water:

- Use a large pot with ample water. Add a generous amount of salt for flavor.

Check Pasta Texture:

- Start testing for doneness a minute or two before the package instructions suggest. Al dente pasta should be firm but not hard.

Reserve Pasta Water:

- Before draining, save a cup of pasta water. This starchy water can be added to the sauce for consistency.

C. Homemade Pasta Options

Egg Pasta:

- Mix 2 cups all-purpose flour with 3 large eggs, knead, and roll out. Cut into desired shapes.

Spinach Pasta:

- Add pureed spinach to the egg and flour mixture for a vibrant, flavorful twist.

Whole Wheat Pasta:

- Substitute part or all of the flour with whole wheat flour for a nutty flavor and added nutrition.

D. Gluten-Free Alternatives

Rice Pasta:

- A gluten-free option that works well with any Bolognese variation.

Quinoa Pasta:

- Provides a protein boost and a unique texture.

Zucchini Noodles (Zoodles):

- For a low-carb, gluten-free alternative, use spiralized zucchini as a base.

Experiment with different pasta shapes and types to find your favorite pairing. Whether you prefer the classics or want to explore healthier or gluten-free options, the perfect pasta enhances the Bolognese experience.

V. Sides and Accompaniments
A. Garlic Bread Varieties

Classic Garlic Bread:

- Slice a baguette, spread a mixture of butter, minced garlic, and parsley, and bake until golden.

Cheesy Garlic Bread:

- Elevate the classic by adding a layer of melted mozzarella or Parmesan on top before baking.

Herb-infused Garlic Bread:

- Mix minced garlic with olive oil, parsley, thyme, and rosemary. Spread on the bread and bake for a fragrant twist.

B. Fresh Salad Ideas

Classic Italian Salad:

- Combine cherry tomatoes, fresh mozzarella, basil leaves, and a drizzle of balsamic glaze.

Arugula and Parmesan Salad:

- Toss arugula with shaved Parmesan, cherry tomatoes, and a lemon vinaigrette.

Caprese Salad Skewers:

- Thread mozzarella balls, cherry tomatoes, and fresh basil leaves onto skewers. Drizzle with balsamic reduction.

C. Wine Pairing Suggestions

Classic Bolognese:

- Pair with a bold red wine such as Chianti, Sangiovese, or a rich Cabernet Sauvignon.

Vegetarian Bolognese:

- Opt for a medium-bodied red wine like Pinot Noir or a red blend.

Seafood Twist:

- Choose a crisp and light white wine, such as Pinot Grigio or Sauvignon Blanc.

Chicken Bolognese:

- Complement the chicken with a white wine like Chardonnay or a light red like Pinot Noir.

Serve the sides family-style for everyone to enjoy. The crunch of garlic bread, the freshness of the salads, and the right wine pairing will enhance the dining experience, making it a complete and satisfying meal.

VI. Creative Bolognese Fusion
A. Bolognese Lasagna

Layering Techniques:

a. Start with a layer of Bolognese sauce at the bottom of the baking dish, ensuring even coverage.

b. Add a layer of lasagna noodles, slightly overlapping to create a solid base.

c. Spread a generous layer of ricotta cheese mixed with one beaten egg and chopped fresh basil. This adds a creamy texture and herbaceous flavor.

d. Repeat the layers, alternating between noodles, Bolognese sauce, and ricotta mixture, finishing with a final layer of Bolognese sauce on top.

e. Sprinkle a blend of shredded mozzarella and grated Parmesan cheese on the top layer for a gooey, golden crust when baked.

Cheese Selection:

- Choose high-quality whole milk ricotta for a creamy texture in the layers.
- Use a combination of mozzarella and Parmesan for a well-balanced, savory flavor profile.

B. Bolognese-Stuffed Peppers

Bell Pepper Varieties:

- Select a variety of bell peppers for a visually appealing dish. The sweetness of red, yellow, and green peppers complements the savory Bolognese.
- Cut the peppers in half lengthwise, creating sturdy vessels for the stuffing.

Baking Tips:

a. Precook the bell peppers in boiling water for about 3-4 minutes to soften them slightly before stuffing.

b. Fill each pepper half with a generous portion of Bolognese sauce, ensuring it's evenly distributed.

c. Top each stuffed pepper with a layer of shredded mozzarella for a melty finish.

d. Bake in the oven until the peppers are tender, and the cheese is bubbly and golden brown.

C. Bolognese Pizza

Pizza Dough Options:

a. For convenience, use store-bought pizza dough. Alternatively, prepare a homemade dough using a mix of all-purpose flour, yeast, olive oil, and water.

b. Roll out the pizza dough to your preferred thickness, creating a thin and crispy crust.

Unique Toppings:

a. Spread a thin layer of Bolognese sauce evenly over the pizza dough, acting as a rich and flavorful pizza sauce.

b. Top with a blend of shredded fontina and provolone cheese for a perfect melt and a combination of nutty and smoky flavors.

c. Enhance the pizza with additional toppings like caramelized onions for sweetness, sliced mushrooms for earthiness, and fresh basil for a burst of freshness.

These creative Bolognese fusions offer a delightful departure from traditional recipes, providing a feast for the senses with layers of flavor and innovative pairings.

VII. Leftover Reinventions
A. Bolognese Stuffed Shells

Ingredients:

- Leftover Bolognese sauce
- Jumbo pasta shells, cooked according to package instructions
- Ricotta cheese
- Shredded mozzarella
- Grated Parmesan
- Fresh basil, chopped

Instructions:

1. Preheat the oven to 375°F (190°C).
2. In a mixing bowl, combine ricotta cheese and a portion of the Bolognese sauce.
3. Stuff each cooked pasta shell with the ricotta and Bolognese mixture.
4. Arrange the stuffed shells in a baking dish.
5. Pour the remaining Bolognese sauce over the shells.
6. Sprinkle shredded mozzarella and grated Parmesan on top.
7. Bake until the cheese is melted and bubbly, usually around 20-25 minutes.
8. Garnish with fresh chopped basil before serving.

B. Bolognese Quesadillas

Ingredients:

- Leftover Bolognese sauce
- Flour tortillas
- Shredded cheddar cheese
- Fresh cilantro, chopped
- Sour cream (for serving)

Instructions:

1. Heat a skillet over medium heat.
2. Place a tortilla in the skillet and spread a layer of Bolognese sauce.
3. Sprinkle shredded cheddar cheese over the sauce.
4. Top with another tortilla and press down gently.
5. Cook until the bottom tortilla is golden brown, then flip and cook the other side.
6. Repeat for additional quesadillas.
7. Once cooked, cut each quesadilla into wedges.
8. Serve with a dollop of sour cream and a sprinkle of fresh cilantro.

C. Bolognese Omelette

Ingredients:

- Leftover Bolognese sauce
- Eggs
- Salt and pepper to taste
- Olive oil or butter for cooking
- Grated Parmesan (optional)
- Fresh parsley, chopped (for garnish)

Instructions:

1. In a bowl, beat eggs and season with salt and pepper.
2. Heat oil or butter in a skillet over medium heat.
3. Pour the beaten eggs into the skillet.
4. Spoon Bolognese sauce over one half of the omelette.
5. Optionally, sprinkle grated Parmesan over the sauce.
6. Once the eggs are set, fold the omelette in half.
7. Cook for an additional minute until the cheese is melted.
8. Slide the omelette onto a plate, garnish with fresh parsley, and serve.

These leftover reinventions provide delicious and creative ways to enjoy Bolognese in new and exciting dishes.

VIII. Troubleshooting and FAQs

A. Common Mistakes to Avoid
Overcooking the Sauce:

- **Issue:** Simmering the Bolognese for too long can result in a dry and overly concentrated sauce.
- **Solution:** Monitor the simmering process and adjust the heat as needed. Add a bit of broth or water if it becomes too thick.

Using Low-Quality Ingredients:

- **Issue:** The quality of meat and tomatoes significantly impacts the flavor.
- **Solution:** Invest in high-quality meats and San Marzano tomatoes for an authentic and rich taste.

Skipping the Browning Step:

- **Issue:** Neglecting to brown the meat and vegetables can lead to a lack of depth in flavor.
- **Solution:** Ensure proper browning during the initial sautéing stage to enhance the overall taste.

B. Adjusting Flavors

Too Salty:

- **Issue:** Over-salting the sauce.
- **Solution:** Add unsalted tomato sauce or diced tomatoes to balance the saltiness. A pinch of sugar can also help.

Lacking Depth:

- **Issue:** The sauce is one-dimensional.
- **Solution:** Increase the cooking time to allow flavors to meld. Add a splash of red wine for complexity.

Too Acidic:

- **Issue:** The sauce is overly tangy.
- **Solution:** Add a pinch of baking soda to neutralize acidity. Alternatively, a touch of honey or sugar can balance the flavors.

C. Storage and Reheating Tips

Refrigerating:

Store leftover Bolognese in airtight containers in the refrigerator for up to 3-4 days.

Freezing:

Portion Bolognese into freezer-safe containers and freeze for up to 3 months.

Reheating:

For refrigerated leftovers, reheat on the stovetop over low heat, adding a splash of broth if needed.

When reheating frozen Bolognese, thaw in the refrigerator overnight and then reheat on the stovetop.

Refreshing Flavors:

Before serving reheated Bolognese, freshen it up with a sprinkle of fresh herbs, a drizzle of olive oil, or a splash of wine.

Pasta Storage:

Store cooked pasta separately from the sauce to prevent it from becoming mushy. Reheat pasta by briefly dipping it in hot water or by sautéing with a bit of olive oil.

By addressing common mistakes, adjusting flavors, and following proper storage and reheating techniques, you can ensure a consistently delicious Bolognese experience.

X. Homemade Pasta from Scratch

A. Basic Pasta Dough Recipe
Ingredients:

- 2 cups all-purpose flour
- 3 large eggs
- Pinch of salt

Instructions:
Create a Mound:

- On a clean surface, make a mound with the flour. Create a well in the center.

Add Eggs:

- Crack the eggs into the well. Add a pinch of salt.

Gradually Combine:

- Using a fork, gradually incorporate the flour into the eggs. Be cautious not to breach the well's walls.

Knead the Dough:

- Once a dough forms, use your hands to knead it for about 10 minutes until smooth and elastic.

Rest the Dough:

- Wrap the dough in plastic wrap and let it rest at room temperature for at least 30 minutes. This allows the gluten to relax.

Roll Out:

- After resting, roll out the dough to your desired thickness using a rolling pin.

B. Rolling and Cutting Techniques

Rolling:

- Divide the rested dough into manageable portions.
- Flour the surface and dough to prevent sticking.
- Roll the dough from the center outwards, turning it occasionally to maintain an even thickness.

Cutting:

- Use a sharp knife or pasta cutter for straight shapes like fettuccine or tagliatelle.
- For stuffed pasta, cut squares or circles for easier folding and sealing.

Using a Pasta Machine:

- If you have a pasta machine, divide the dough into smaller pieces.
- Flatten each piece and feed it through the machine on the widest setting.
- Gradually decrease the thickness until achieving the desired thinness.

C. Unique Pasta Shapes for Bolognese

Pappardelle:

- Wide, ribbon-like pasta that pairs well with hearty Bolognese.

Orecchiette:

- Small, ear-shaped pasta that captures the sauce in its concave center.

Maltagliati:

- Irregularly shaped pasta squares, perfect for a rustic Bolognese.

Garganelli:

- Rolled pasta resembling small cylinders that catch the sauce effectively.

Trofie:

- Twisted, short pasta ideal for clinging onto thick Bolognese.

Corzetti:

- Decorative pasta discs stamped with intricate designs, offering a unique presentation.

Homemade pasta adds a personal touch to your Bolognese experience. Experiment with different shapes to enhance the overall texture and presentation of your dish.

XI. Bolognese for Every Diet
A. Keto-Friendly Bolognese

Low-Carb Ingredients:

- **Ground Meat Selection:**

Choose high-quality, fatty cuts of ground beef and pork.
Optionally, incorporate ground veal for a more luxurious texture.

- **Aromatic Vegetables:**

Use moderate amounts of onion and garlic for flavor without excessive carbs.
Limit celery to a small amount, as it contains fewer carbs than other vegetables.

- **Tomato Varieties:**

Opt for crushed tomatoes in moderation, or use tomato paste for a concentrated flavor with fewer carbs.

- **Herbs and Spices:**

Emphasize keto-friendly herbs like basil, oregano, thyme, and rosemary.
Consider using bay leaves for added depth.

- **Alternative Sweeteners:**

If a touch of sweetness is desired, use keto-friendly sweeteners like erythritol or stevia in small amounts.

Substituting Pasta with Vegetables:

- **Zucchini Noodles (Zoodles):**

Spiralize fresh zucchini into noodle-like shapes. Saute briefly for an al dente texture.

- **Spaghetti Squash:**

Roast or microwave spaghetti squash until tender. Scrape out the strands with a fork.

- **Shirataki Noodles:**

Rinse and prepare shirataki noodles according to package instructions for a virtually carb-free option.

B. Gluten-Free Bolognese

Alternative Grains and Flours:

- **Gluten-Free Flour:**

Use a gluten-free all-purpose flour blend to thicken the Bolognese, maintaining a similar texture.

- **Alternative Grains:**

Consider serving Bolognese over gluten-free grains like quinoa or rice as a delicious accompaniment.

- **Tamari or Gluten-Free Soy Sauce:**

Replace traditional soy sauce with tamari, which is gluten-free but imparts the same umami flavor.

- **Cornstarch or Arrowroot:**

Thicken the sauce using cornstarch or arrowroot powder instead of wheat-based flours.

Tips for Gluten-Free Pasta:

- **Rice Pasta:**

Select rice-based pasta for a gluten-free alternative that closely resembles the texture of traditional pasta.

- **Corn Pasta:**

Explore corn-based pasta for a unique flavor profile that complements the richness of Bolognese.

- **Almond Flour Pasta:**

Experiment with almond flour-based pasta for a nutty and hearty gluten-free option.

- **Gluten-Free Precautions:**

Always check labels to ensure all ingredients, including spices and condiments, are gluten-free to avoid cross-contamination.

Adapting Bolognese for keto and gluten-free diets involves thoughtful ingredient selection and creative pasta alternatives, allowing everyone to savor this classic dish while adhering to their dietary preferences.

XII. International Bolognese Inspirations
A. Bolognese with Mediterranean Flavors

Olives, Capers, and Feta:

- **Ingredients:**

Alongside traditional Bolognese ingredients, add pitted Kalamata olives and capers for a briny kick.
Finish with crumbled feta cheese for a tangy and savory element.

- **Cooking Techniques:**

Stir in olives and capers during the simmering process to allow their flavors to meld.
Sprinkle feta on top just before serving for a creamy contrast.

- **Serving Suggestions:**

Serve over al dente tagliatelle or pappardelle for a Mediterranean twist.

Lighter Olive Oil Base:

- **Ingredients:**

Replace some or all of the traditional olive oil with extra virgin olive oil for a fresher taste.

- **Cooking Techniques:**

Add the extra virgin olive oil towards the end of the cooking process to preserve its vibrant flavor.

- **Serving Suggestions:**

Pair with a light, crisp white wine, such as Pinot Grigio, to complement the Mediterranean flavors.

B. Asian Fusion Bolognese

Soy Sauce and Ginger Infusion:

- **Ingredients:**

Introduce soy sauce, fresh ginger, and a dash of sesame oil for an Asian-inspired flavor profile.

- **Cooking Techniques:**

Infuse soy sauce and ginger during the sautéing stage to permeate the meat with Asian flavors.
Add a touch of sesame oil towards the end for a delightful finish.

- **Serving Suggestions:**

Pair with rice noodles or udon noodles to enhance the Asian fusion experience.

Rice Noodle Pairing:

- **Ingredients:**

Serve the Asian-inspired Bolognese over cooked rice noodles or rice for a gluten-free option.

- **Cooking Techniques:**

Cook rice noodles separately according to package instructions and toss them with the Asian Bolognese just before serving.

- **Serving Suggestions:**

Garnish with chopped green onions and cilantro for a burst of freshness.

C. Southwestern Bolognese

Spices and Chili Peppers:

- **Ingredients:**

Enhance the Bolognese with Southwestern spices like cumin, coriander, and chili powder.
Introduce diced green chilies or jalapeños for heat.

- **Cooking Techniques:**

Incorporate the spices early in the cooking process to allow them to meld with the meat.
Add diced chilies towards the end for a bold, spicy kick.

- **Serving Suggestions:**

Serve over corn-based dishes like polenta or cornbread to complement the Southwestern flavors.
Corn-Based Side Dishes:

- **Ingredients:**

Accompany the Southwestern Bolognese with corn-based sides like polenta, cornbread, or corn tortillas.

- **Cooking Techniques:**

Prepare corn-based sides according to your preference and serve alongside the flavorful Bolognese.

- **Serving Suggestions:**

Garnish with fresh cilantro and a dollop of sour cream for a Southwestern touch.

These international Bolognese inspirations showcase the versatility of the classic sauce, allowing you to explore different culinary traditions and flavors.

XIII. Bolognese and Beyond: Sauces for All Seasons

A. Summer Bolognese with Fresh Garden Ingredients
   Seasonal Vegetables:

- **Ingredients:**

Incorporate fresh, seasonal vegetables like zucchini, cherry tomatoes, and bell peppers.
Add a handful of basil and mint for a burst of summer freshness.

- **Cooking Techniques:**

Sauté the vegetables briefly to maintain their vibrant colors and crisp texture.
Toss in fresh herbs towards the end to preserve their aromatic qualities.

- **Serving Suggestions:**

Serve the Summer Bolognese over light and airy pasta like angel hair or serve it with a side of grilled vegetables.
   Lighter, Tomato-Free Variation:

- **Ingredients:**

Instead of tomatoes, use a combination of vegetable or chicken broth to maintain moisture.
Enhance the flavor with a squeeze of lemon juice for brightness.

- **Cooking Techniques:**

Simmer the sauce until the broth reduces slightly, concentrating the flavors.

Finish with a touch of lemon juice just before serving.

- **Serving Suggestions:**

Pair with a chilled white wine and a side of crusty bread for a delightful summer meal.

B. Cozy Fall Bolognese with Harvest Flavors

Pumpkin and Butternut Squash Additions:

- **Ingredients:**

Introduce diced butternut squash or pumpkin for a rich, sweet flavor. Use a hint of nutmeg or cinnamon to enhance the fall-inspired profile.

- **Cooking Techniques:**

Sauté the squash until it begins to caramelize, adding a depth of flavor.
Sprinkle nutmeg or cinnamon sparingly to avoid overpowering the dish.

- **Serving Suggestions:**

Serve over wide egg noodles or gnocchi to complement the comforting fall flavors.

Comforting Herbs and Spices:

- **Ingredients:**

Incorporate warming herbs like sage and rosemary.
Use ground cloves or allspice for a subtle hint of warmth.

- **Cooking Techniques:**

Add the herbs and spices during the initial sautéing stage to infuse the sauce with their comforting aromas.

Simmer the sauce until it thickens, allowing the flavors to meld.

- **Serving Suggestions:**

Enjoy with a glass of red wine and a side of garlic mashed potatoes for a hearty fall meal.

C. Winter Warmer Bolognese

Rich, Hearty Ingredients:

- **Ingredients:**

Choose hearty meats like a mix of beef and pork or even lamb for a robust flavor.

Include root vegetables such as carrots and parsnips for additional depth.

- **Cooking Techniques:**

Brown the meats thoroughly to develop a rich, caramelized flavor. Simmer the sauce slowly to allow the flavors to meld and intensify.

- **Serving Suggestions:**

Serve over pappardelle or rigatoni for a satisfying winter meal.
Red Wine Reduction:

- **Ingredients:**

Use a generous amount of red wine to create a luxurious reduction. Add a touch of balsamic vinegar for acidity and depth.

- **Cooking Techniques:**

Deglaze the pan with red wine after browning the meat, scraping up flavorful bits from the bottom.

Allow the sauce to simmer until the wine reduces, creating a luscious, concentrated flavor.

- **Serving Suggestions:**

Pair with a bold red wine and serve alongside a rustic loaf of crusty bread.

These Bolognese variations embrace the flavors of each season, providing a comforting and satisfying experience year-round.

XIV. Quick and Easy Bolognese Weeknight Meals

A. One-Pot Bolognese

Simplified Ingredients:

- **Ingredients:**

Lean ground beef or turkey for quicker cooking.
Pre-chopped mirepoix (carrots, celery, and onion) or use frozen diced vegetables.
Crushed tomatoes or tomato sauce for convenience.
Dried herbs like oregano and basil for quick seasoning.

- **Cooking Techniques:**

Brown the meat in the pot first, then add the pre-chopped vegetables.
Skip the lengthy simmering time by using tomato sauce instead of whole tomatoes.

- **Time-Saving Tips:**

Opt for pre-packaged, pre-chopped vegetables for even faster preparation.
Consider using a leaner ground meat, as it cooks more quickly.

B. 30-Minute Bolognese Recipes

Express Cooking Techniques:

* **Ingredients:**

Ground beef or turkey for quick cooking.
Pre-made marinara or Bolognese sauce as a base.
Instant umami boost with Worcestershire sauce or soy sauce.

* **Cooking Techniques:**

Brown the meat quickly, then add the pre-made sauce.
Enhance the flavor with Worcestershire sauce or soy sauce for depth.

* **Time-Saving Tips:**

Choose a high-quality pre-made sauce to cut down on cooking time.
Utilize pre-cooked or par-cooked pasta for an even faster meal.
Prepping in Advance:

* **Ingredients:**

Make a batch of Bolognese sauce ahead of time and freeze in portions.
Keep pre-cooked pasta or fresh pasta in the refrigerator.

* **Cooking Techniques:**

Thaw the pre-made Bolognese sauce in the microwave or on the stovetop.
Cook the pasta while reheating the sauce.

- **Time-Saving Tips:**

Pre-portion and freeze Bolognese sauce for quick access on busy nights.

Consider using fresh pasta, which cooks faster than dried pasta.

These quick and easy Bolognese weeknight meals are designed for efficiency without compromising on flavor. Whether using shortcuts or prepping in advance, you can enjoy a satisfying Bolognese on even the busiest evenings.

XV. Bolognese Brunch Delights

A. Bolognese Benedict

Poached Eggs and Hollandaise:

- **Ingredients:**

Fresh poached eggs for a runny yolk.
Classic hollandaise sauce or a quick blender hollandaise.

- **Assembly:**

Toast English muffins and place a generous portion of reheated Bolognese on each half.
Top with a perfectly poached egg.

- **Garnish:**

Drizzle hollandaise over the eggs.
Garnish with freshly chopped chives for a burst of freshness.
English Muffin Base:

- **Ingredients:**

English muffins, toasted to perfection.

- **Assembly:**

Use toasted English muffins as the sturdy base for the Bolognese Benedict.
The nooks and crannies of the muffin absorb the flavors of the Bolognese.

- **Garnish:**

Garnish with a sprinkle of flaky sea salt and a twist of freshly ground black pepper.

B. Bolognese Breakfast Burritos

Scrambled Eggs and Cheese:

- **Ingredients:**

Fluffy scrambled eggs seasoned with salt and pepper.
A blend of shredded cheddar and Monterey Jack cheese.

- **Assembly:**

Warm flour tortillas and spoon a portion of Bolognese onto each.
Add a layer of scrambled eggs and a generous sprinkle of cheese.

- **Wrap and Roll:**

Fold in the sides of the tortilla and roll it up tightly.
Place the burritos seam-side down in a heated skillet to crisp up the tortilla.

Wrap Varieties:

- **Ingredients:**

Explore different tortilla varieties, such as spinach, whole wheat, or tomato-flavored.

- **Assembly:**

Experiment with alternative wraps for a unique flavor dimension.
Choose wraps that complement the Bolognese and add a touch of color.

- **Garnish:**

Garnish with a dollop of sour cream, a drizzle of hot sauce, and a sprinkle of fresh cilantro.

These Bolognese brunch delights add a savory twist to classic breakfast items. Whether enjoying the elegance of Bolognese Benedict or the portability of Bolognese breakfast burritos, these dishes make brunch a delightful and satisfying experience.

XVI. Healthy Bolognese for Kids

A. Sneaky Veggie Incorporation
Vegetable Puree:

- **Ingredients:**

Blend carrots, celery, and bell peppers into a smooth puree.
Add the puree to the Bolognese sauce for added nutrition.

- **Cooking Techniques:**

Sauté the vegetable puree with the ground meat, allowing it to blend
seamlessly into the sauce.
Simmer the sauce until the puree is fully incorporated.

- **Presentation:**

Kids won't notice the hidden veggies, and the Bolognese will have a
rich, colorful appearance.

B. Kid-Friendly Pasta Shapes

Fun Pasta Varieties:

- **Ingredients:**

Choose pasta shapes that appeal to kids, such as wagon wheels, animal shapes, or colorful pasta.

- **Cooking Techniques:**

Cook pasta according to package instructions until al dente.
Fun shapes make the meal visually appealing and exciting for kids.

- **Presentation:**

Serve Bolognese over the playful pasta shapes to make mealtime enjoyable and engaging.

C. Tips for Getting Children Involved in Cooking

1. Veggie Prep Fun:

- **Involvement:**

Have kids help wash, peel, and chop vegetables (under supervision). Allow them to add the vegetable puree to the sauce and stir.
Choose Their Pasta:

- **Involvement:**

Let kids pick their favorite pasta shapes for the meal.
They can assist in adding the pasta to boiling water and stirring occasionally.
Set the Table Together:

- **Involvement:**

Involve children in setting the table with plates, napkins, and utensils.
This fosters a sense of accomplishment and responsibility.
Tasting and Adjusting:

- **Involvement:**

Encourage kids to taste and adjust seasoning with your guidance.
This helps develop their palate and a sense of ownership in the meal.
Create a Bolognese Pizza Night:

- **Involvement:**

Transform Bolognese night into a pizza-making event.

Allow kids to spread Bolognese on pizza dough and add their favorite toppings.

By incorporating veggies into the Bolognese, choosing kid-friendly pasta shapes, and involving children in the cooking process, you create a healthy and enjoyable meal that encourages kids to explore new flavors and become more connected to their food.

XVII. Bolognese Desserts

A. Savory-Sweet Combinations
Bolognese-Infused Savory-Sweet Sauce:

- **Ingredients:**

Cook down Bolognese sauce until it thickens into a savory-sweet glaze.

Add a touch of honey or balsamic reduction to enhance the sweetness.

- **Pairing:**

Drizzle the savory-sweet Bolognese sauce over vanilla ice cream or panna cotta.

The contrast of sweet and savory flavors creates a unique dessert experience.

Candied Bacon Bolognese Topping:

- **Ingredients:**

Candy bacon in the oven with brown sugar.
Crumble the candied bacon as a crunchy, sweet topping.

- **Pairing:**

Sprinkle the candied bacon over a chocolate or caramel dessert.
The sweet-savory crunch adds a surprising twist.

B. Bolognese-Infused Dessert Ideas

Bolognese Chocolate Truffles:

- **Ingredients:**

Mix Bolognese sauce with dark chocolate ganache.
Roll the mixture into truffle-sized balls.

- **Coating:**

Roll the truffles in cocoa powder or chopped nuts for texture.
Chill until firm and serve as an unexpected dessert.
Bolognese Berry Compote:

- **Ingredients:**

Cook down Bolognese with a mix of berries (strawberries, raspberries, blueberries).
Sweeten with a touch of sugar or honey.

- **Pairing:**

Spoon the berry-Bolognese compote over cheesecake or vanilla ice cream.
The fruity sweetness balances the savory undertones.
Bolognese Parfait:

- **Layering:**

Alternate layers of Bolognese sauce with vanilla or honey-flavored yogurt.
Top with granola or nuts for added texture.

- **Presentation:**

Serve in clear glasses to showcase the beautiful layers.
A visually appealing and unexpected dessert option.

Experimenting with savory-sweet combinations and incorporating Bolognese into dessert opens up a world of culinary creativity. These dessert ideas bring a delightful twist to the traditional notion of Bolognese, surprising and satisfying your taste buds.

XVIII. Bolognese and Beverage Pairing

A. Craft Beer Recommendations
Rich and Malty Ale:

- **Flavor Profile:**

Choose a malty ale with caramel and toasty notes.
The maltiness complements the richness of the Bolognese.

- **Recommendation:**

English-style Brown Ale or a malty Amber Ale.
Hoppy IPA:

- **Flavor Profile:**

An IPA with a strong hop profile can cut through the richness of the Bolognese.
Look for citrusy or piney hop characteristics.

- **Recommendation:**

American IPA or a West Coast IPA.
Robust Stout:

- Flavor Profile:

A stout with roasted malt flavors enhances the meatiness of the Bolognese.
The creaminess of a stout can complement the sauce.

- **Recommendation:**

Irish Dry Stout or American Stout.

B. Non-Alcoholic Pairing Options

Sparkling Water with Citrus:

- **Flavor Profile:**

Crisp sparkling water with a splash of lemon or lime.
Refreshing and palate-cleansing.

- **Presentation:**

Serve in a tall glass with ice and a citrus wedge.
Iced Herbal Tea:

- **Flavor Profile:**

Choose a caffeine-free herbal tea like peppermint or chamomile.
The herbal notes provide a soothing contrast.

- **Presentation:**

Serve over ice with a sprig of fresh mint.

C. Bolognese-inspired Cocktails

Bolognese Mary:

- **Ingredients:**

Vodka, tomato juice, Worcestershire sauce, hot sauce.
Garnish with a celery stick and a small spoonful of Bolognese.

- **Flavor Profile:**

A savory twist on the classic Bloody Mary, the Bolognese adds depth.
Red Wine Spritzer:

- **Ingredients:**

Red wine, soda water, a splash of Bolognese reduction.
Garnish with an orange slice.

- **Flavor Profile:**

A refreshing wine cocktail with a hint of Bolognese richness.
Bolognese-infused Martini:

- **Ingredients:**

Gin or vodka, dry vermouth, a splash of Bolognese reduction.
Garnish with a twist of lemon.

- **Flavor Profile:**

A sophisticated martini with a savory twist from the Bolognese reduction.

Pairing beverages with Bolognese involves finding flavors that complement or contrast with the rich and savory elements of the sauce. Craft beers, non-alcoholic options, and Bolognese-inspired cocktails all provide exciting choices to enhance your dining experience.

XIX. Mastering the Art of Leftover Storage

A. Freezing Bolognese for Later

1. Portion Control:

- Divide the Bolognese into meal-sized portions before freezing.
- Use airtight containers or heavy-duty freezer bags for storage.

2. Labeling:

- Clearly label each container with the date and type of Bolognese.
- This ensures you use the oldest batches first for optimal freshness.

3. Freeze Flat:

- Lay freezer bags flat during freezing for easy stacking and efficient use of freezer space.
- This method also allows for quicker thawing.

4. Leave Room for Expansion:

- If using containers, leave a bit of space at the top to accommodate expansion as the Bolognese freezes.

B. Creative Reheating Techniques

Stovetop Simmer:

- Thaw Bolognese in the refrigerator or use the defrost function in the microwave.
- Reheat on the stovetop, adding a splash of broth or wine to rejuvenate flavors.

Oven Baked:

- Transfer thawed Bolognese to an oven-safe dish.
- Bake in the oven at a low temperature, covered, to prevent drying out.

Slow Cooker Magic:

- Place frozen Bolognese directly into a slow cooker.
- Cook on low for several hours, allowing the flavors to meld.

Microwave Shortcut:

- For a quick individual serving, microwave frozen Bolognese in short intervals, stirring in between.

C. Building New Meals from Frozen Leftovers

Bolognese Stuffed Vegetables:

- Use frozen Bolognese to stuff bell peppers, zucchini, or large mushrooms.
- Bake until the vegetables are tender, creating a new and exciting dish.

Bolognese Calzone:

- Thaw Bolognese and drain excess liquid.
- Use as a savory filling for homemade or store-bought pizza dough, creating a delicious Bolognese calzone.

Bolognese Baked Potatoes:

- Bake or microwave potatoes until tender.
- Reheat Bolognese and spoon over split baked potatoes, adding cheese and other toppings.

Bolognese Quesadilla:

- Spread thawed Bolognese between tortillas with cheese.
- Cook in a skillet until the tortillas are crispy, creating a flavorful Bolognese quesadilla.

Mastering leftover storage involves careful freezing, creative reheating techniques, and transforming frozen Bolognese into exciting new meals. With a bit of ingenuity, you can turn leftovers into delightful and varied culinary experiences.

IX. Conclusion

A. Celebrating the Versatility of Bolognese

In concluding our culinary journey through the world of Bolognese, we celebrate the remarkable versatility of this timeless sauce. From its humble origins in the heart of Italy to the kitchens around the globe, Bolognese has transcended borders and become a canvas for creativity and innovation.

Through the exploration of classic recipes and inventive variations, we've discovered the endless possibilities that Bolognese offers. Whether enjoyed over traditional pasta, as a stuffing, or even as part of unexpected desserts, Bolognese has proven itself to be a culinary chameleon, adapting to diverse tastes and preferences.

B. Encouragement for Culinary Exploration

As we bid farewell to this culinary journey, let this be an encouragement for continued culinary exploration. Bolognese has shown us that the joy of cooking lies not just in following recipes but in experimenting, adapting, and making each dish uniquely our own. Whether you're a seasoned chef or a novice in the kitchen, let Bolognese inspire you to embrace the artistry of cooking.

So, let the simmering pots, the aroma-filled kitchens, and the shared meals with loved ones be a testament to the joy that cooking brings. May your future culinary adventures be filled with discovery, creativity, and the sheer pleasure of savoring the fruits of your labor.

Thank you for joining us on this delightful journey through the world of Bolognese. Happy cooking, and may your kitchen be forever filled with the rich and comforting essence of this beloved sauce. Buon appetito!

9 798223 269281